MEDIEVAL KNIGHTS

DAVID NICOLLE

VIKING

Acknowledgments

The publishers would like to thank Bill Donohoe and Terry Gabbey, who illustrated the see-through scenes; James Field, who illustrated the cover; and the individuals and organizations that have given their permission to reproduce the following pictures:

Ancient Art & Architecture Collection: 11 top left, 16 top left, 36 top right, 37 top right.
Antikvarisk-Topografiska-Arkivet: 35 center right.
Biblioteca Apostolica Vaticana: 4 below right.
Bibliothéque Nationale, Paris: 17 center right.
Board of Trustees of the Royal Armouries: 29 bottom right.
Bodleian Library, Oxford: 35 bottom right.
British Library: 14 top left, 31 bottom right (both), 44 top left.
Crown copyright: reproduction by permission of Historic Scotland: 45 top right.
J. Allan Cash: 27 top left, 37 center left. Michael Dixon: 43 center right. **Edinburgh University Library, Kelvingrove:** 38 bottom right, 39 top right.
Glasgow Museums & Art Gallery: 45 bottom right.
Kremlin: 38 bottom left. **Kunsthistorisches Museum, Wien:** 7 top left (both).
Masters & Fellows of Trinity College, Cambridge: 9 top right.
Michael Holford: 25 top right. **Museo d'Arte de Barcelona:** 41 top right.
National Museum, Budapest: 12 bottom right.
The Pierpont Morgan Library: 34 top left.
Scala: 7 top right, 10 bottom right, 15 center left, 19 bottom right, 19 bottom left, 20 bottom right, 22 bottom right, 23 top right, 23 bottom right, 27 bottom right, 43 bottom left.
Sonia Halliday: 30 top left, 32 center right. **Southampton City Heritage Services:** 27 top right.
Warburg-Stiflung: 21 top right. **Dr D. Winfield:** 28 bottom right.

Illustrators:
Johnathan Adams: icons, 5, 12, 18, 26 top, 29. **James Field (Simon Girling):** cover.
Terry Gabbey (Associated Freelance Artists): 6, 7, 13 bottom, 19, 22, 30, 31, 35.
André Hrydziuszko: 6 top, 15 bottom, 16 bottom, 38. **Angus McBride (Linden Artists):** title page, 4, 13 top, 14, 15, 26-27, 28, 34, 39, 42, 44-45, 46-47. **Mike White:** 10-11, 16-17, 20, 21, 36, 37, 43.

VIKING
Published by the Penguin Group
Penguin Books USA Inc., 375 Hudson Street, New York, New York 10014, U.S.A.
Penguin Books Ltd, 27 Wrights Lane, London W8 5TZ, England
Penguin Books Australia Ltd, Ringwood, Victoria, Australia
Penguin Books Canada Ltd, 10 Alcorn Avenue, Toronto, Ontario, Canada M4V 3B2
Penguin Books (N.Z.) Ltd, 182–190 Wairau Road, Auckland 10, New Zealand

Penguin Books Ltd, Registered Offices: Harmondsworth, Middlesex, England

First published in Great Britain by Heinemann Children's Reference,
a division of Reed Educational & Professional Publishing Ltd., 1997
First published in the United States of America by Viking,
a division of Penguin Books USA Inc., 1997

1   3   5   7   9   10   8   6   4   2

Copyright © Reed Educational & Professional Publishing Ltd., 1997

Library of Congress Catalog Card Number: 96-61599

ISBN 0-670-87463-9

Printed in Italy

CONTENTS

Most people think of the Middle Ages as a time when brave warriors and heroic knights in shining armor killed dragons and rescued damsels in distress. In reality, knights were often ordinary men—soldiers in the service of a wealthy lord or leader—who fought to defend their king, their country, Christianity, or their honor.

In the story of Sir Gawain and the Green Knight, the giant returns after a year and a day to deal Gawain a single blow, as they had agreed upon in their duel. As a true knight, Gawain prepares to meet the challenge, though it will mean his death. But the Green Knight respects Gawain's honorable behavior, and so lets him live.

ARTHURIAN LEGENDS

Among the most famous stories of medieval knights are the Arthurian legends, which tell of the adventures of a fabled fifth century warrior-king named Arthur and his elite band of loyal knights—the Knights of the Round Table. One of the knights was Sir Lancelot, who betrayed his knightly vows by falling in love with Guinevere, Arthur's queen. Another was Arthur's nephew, Sir Gawain.

SIR GAWAIN AND THE GREEN KNIGHT

Stories about knights were often embellished with accounts of magic or sorcery. According to legend, Sir Gawain accepted a challenge from a giant Green Knight. Gawain was granted the first blow, but if he failed to kill the Green Knight, the giant would return in a year and a day to seek his revenge. Gawain cut off the giant's head, only to discover the Green Knight was a magical creature who could speak even though he held his severed head in his own hands!

This medieval manuscript shows crusader knights besieging the great city of Antioch in A.D. 1098. The popular view of medieval knights is one of brave warriors who were polite to women and respected a brave foe. In reality, knights behaved just like other soldiers.

This map shows the main Christian lands in Europe in about A.D. 1270. Their main neighbors were the Islamic nations to the south and southeast, and the Mongol Golden Horde to the east. By the end of the Middle Ages, Europeans had a clearer idea what the rest of the world contained. Traveling merchants brought back news from as far away as China and perhaps Japan.

LEGENDARY HEROES

Where did these stories of knights and magical creatures originate? In the Middle Ages, there were no radios, televisions, or movies. Instead, poems and songs were used to entertain people. Some of the most imaginative stories were written at this time. Medieval bards and minstrels told tales of the heroism of the knights, and, of course, exaggerated the deeds of their heroes to make the stories more entertaining.

MYTH AND REALITY

Some of these stories show that most Europeans thought the rest of the world a frightening and hostile place. This was mainly because they knew so little about it. They saw knights as the civilized world's defense against the unknown.

Encouraged by the Church, knights went on crusades, fighting Muslims and other non-Christians. They often traveled widely. Caught up in the spirit of "internationalism," men fought beyond the frontiers of Christian Europe. As a result, more information about other parts of the world gradually filtered back to Europe.

Although they feared their neighbors, medieval Europeans were also curious and willing to learn about them. In the *chansons de geste*, epic and heroic songs sung by medieval minstrels, for example, Muslim Saracen soldiers were often described as "knights," just like those of western Europe.

THE DECLINE OF KNIGHTHOOD

The knights played a great part in changing the European view of the medieval world. Gradually, however, western European civilization itself changed, and the knight in armor, as well as the old ideals of knighthood, became outdated and slowly disappeared.

This map shows how most European people viewed the world in about A.D. 1095. "Christendom" was a small part of the medieval world and often felt threatened by its neighbors. Information about these peoples slowly filtered back to Europe, but almost always made these mysterious kingdoms seem much more powerful than they really were. Many people still believed that terrifying sea monsters and strange half-human creatures lived at the edges of the world.

THE FIRST KNIGHTS

THE FIRST KNIGHTS

In the late eighth century, the Holy Roman Empire was created by Charlemagne, king of the Franks. To build and defend his new empire, Charlemagne needed thousands of well-trained professional soldiers. At the very top of his army were armored cavalrymen who were in many ways the first knights of medieval Europe. The armies led by Charlemagne and his successors were also the only ones able to defeat the Vikings who raided northwest Europe in the ninth and tenth centuries.

The early knights lived in castles like the early 11th-century upper fortress that stood in Rüdesheim in Germany.

In the fifth century, the western half of the Roman Empire was destroyed by invading Germanic tribes. Powerful local lords and war-chiefs offered protection to the peasants in return for service, giving rise to a feudal society.

Charles, King of the Franks . . . controlled Rome, where the ancient Caesars had always lived, as well as ruling many other parts of Italy, France, and Germany. So, as God had given him these territories, it seemed right that he should also accept the title of Emperor when it was offered to him by all Christendom.

— The Lauresheim Chronicle —

Charlemagne became emperor with the blessing of the Pope in Rome. He was the first western emperor since the fall of Rome, and his large, efficient army made him the equal of the only other great powers in Europe—the Byzantine Empire in eastern Europe, and the Muslim Caliphate of Spain.

The heavily armored and highly mobile cavalry of Charlemagne's empire led the armies of his successors, the Carolingian and Ottonian emperors. They were the only soldiers able to defeat the Vikings who raided Europe from the north, the Hungarians who invaded from the east, and the Saracens who came from the south.

The early knights fought with spears and swords (right). Their armor usually consisted of chainmail, and iron helmets, like the one above.

CHARLEMAGNE'S KNIGHTS

Charlemagne's cavalrymen wore chainmail armor, an iron helmet, and carried a large wooden shield. They fought with a spear, sword, and sometimes a bow. This equipment was so effective that it hardly changed for 300 years.

However, outfitting a knight and his powerful war-horse was very expensive. The knights had to live all over western Europe if they were to defend every area from invaders. They alone were able to defend the people of western Europe from waves of barbaric Vikings, Magyar Hungarians, and Mediterranean Muslim raiders who almost destroyed the huge and wealthy empire that Charlemagne had created.

FEUDALISM

The development of feudalism helped to sustain the knightly class. A local lord, noble, or other leader would grant land to a knight in return for his military service and loyalty. Peasants, in turn, were afforded protection by the knights and local lords, but worked hard to serve them by feeding them with their crops and by paying hefty taxes.

This kind of military aristocracy gradually elevated the role of knights from mere soldiers to members of a new and powerful ruling class.

THE NORMANS

Perhaps the most effective of the new knights were the Normans—who were themselves descended from a powerful group of Vikings who had settled in Normandy in northwest France. The Normans learned much about warfare from Charlemagne's armies and won many battles through careful planning and daring attacks. They established states in southern Italy and Sicily, and conquered much of Great Britain.

Many Normans also served in the Byzantine armies, and when Pope Urban II called for a crusade against the Muslims, Norman knights from France and Italy were at the forefront of the great armies that went to the Holy Land.

A picture of a Carolingian warrior nobleman (above) found on a small wall-painting in Italy.

The Pope gives Charlemagne a splendidly decorated banner (below) as a sign that he has the Church's support.

ARMING A KNIGHT

Below, a late 12th-century knight and his son are being armed for battle, assisted by two squires. The knights' armor consisted of chainmail—sheets of interlocking iron rings—mostly worn over some sort of quilted padding that absorbed the shock of a blow. When the see-through page is turned, they are shown almost ready for battle.

The arms and armor used by knights and other western European fighting men changed a great deal during the Middle Ages. However, from the earliest days, armor nearly always consisted of more than one layer. The first layer would be a pair of loose breeches and a shirt. Over the breeches the knight would wear hose, which were like two separate tight-fitting trouser legs.

12th-CENTURY KNIGHTS

Over his hose, a 12th-century knight wore mail leggings, called *chausses*. Next, to cushion his armor, he would put on a padded coat called a *gambeson*. On top of this would be a tunic, probably very long as a mark of wealth and status.

12th-CENTURY KNIGHTS

1 Breeches
2 Shirt
3 Hose
4 Chainmail chausses
5 Long tunic
6 Chainmail hauberk
7 Coif over padding
8 Surcoat
9 Helmet

READY FOR BATTLE

The knight's main piece of armor was a chainmail shirt called a *hauberk*, which usually had a chainmail hood called a *coif*. The hauberk was very awkward to put on. Over this would be worn a long cloth surcoat. Short surcoats were known as *gipons*.

Finally, the knight had a helmet, called a *basinet*, to protect his head, and a wooden shield. Armed with a heavy sword for cutting rather than stabbing, and a long lance, the knight was a dangerous enemy.

Below, two knights from around 1325–1350 are taking off their armor after a tournament. Although some of their armor still consists of mail, they also now wear more rigid plate armor made of scales and small pieces of plate. When the see-through page is turned, the basic shirt and padded arming cap worn under the armor can be seen.

PLATE ARMOR

In the 14th century, the lower layers of clothing and armor were similar to those worn earlier, but the knight had extra protection on his arms, elbows, legs, knees, and feet. The strongest item of armor was now plate armor, made of metal scales and plate covered in decorative cloth. A knight's lady might give him a "favor" to wear on his helmet during a tournament; perhaps a piece of colored cloth or even an item of clothing!

14th-CENTURY KNIGHTS

10 Plate armor
11 Surcoat
12 Arm plates
13 Leg plates
14 Helmet

15 Coif over arming cap
16 Padded arming cap
17 Shirt
18 Lance

Armorers were among the most skilled and highly paid craftsmen in the Middle Ages. They formed some of the first guilds, which were a bit like trade unions. They made arms and armor that not only protected the knight, but was often also very beautiful.

BECOMING A KNIGHT

Many medieval manuscripts show knights charging at a piece of equipment called a quintain. Just how it really helped train a knight remains a bit of a mystery!

In the early days knighting, or "dubbing," a knight meant that a military leader gave his knights the arms, armor, and horses that they needed to carry out their duties. But by the 13th century, knighting had become an elaborate ceremony, usually with a strong religious feel.

SQUIRES

In the 12th and 13th centuries, knighthood was a military way of life. Being knighted did not mean a man's military status or position in society was fixed, or that his descendants would be knights. If a soldier did not have the necessary equipment or was not wealthy enough to afford it, he simply could not be a knight.

The first step to becoming a knight was to become a squire. Squires might be the sons of other knights, or the sons of nobles. Starting at about the age of ten, they had to learn all the skills of knighthood. These included how to use and care for weapons, how to ride and look after a horse, and how to fight alongside other knights as part of a team.

ELABORATE CEREMONIES

When a squire had learned these skills, he could become a knight. His lord gave him land to live on. In return he promised to defend his lands and the Church, and to fight in his lord's army.

By the 14th century, the ceremony promoting a squire to the rank of knight could be long and elaborate. If a young squire was from an important family, he would probably have to pray alone all night in church, wearing special clothes to show he was humble before God. Then there was a formal religious ceremony followed by a magnificent feast. More often, several squires would go through simpler versions of these ceremonies as a group.

In the 12th century, a knighting, or dubbing, ceremony could be carried out in camp before a battle or a siege. In this simple and old-fashioned form of knighting, the Church played a minor role, perhaps with a monk simply blessing the men and their weapons.

Hunting in the forests around a castle formed an essential part of a knight's military training. It polished his riding skills, trained him to use cover, to understand the layout of the land, and to cooperate with other huntsmen. Some types of hunting involved the same weapons used in battle.

THE CHURCH'S ROLE

The Church had not always been involved in the knighting ceremony. Once the Vikings and other threats had been defeated, the knights of western Europe found that they now had a

lot of military power. The result was chaos in many parts of Europe as knights fought for kings, barons, or simply for their own profit.

During the 11th and 12th centuries the Church tried to control these troublesome soldiers. If they became "Christian warriors," they were offered a chance of a place in heaven in return. Not only could the knights join the ruling class, but they could also save their souls. To increase its influence over the knights, the Church began to play a bigger role in the knighting ceremony. Swords, once blessed to bring luck or ward off evil, were now seen as versions of the Christian cross that should only be used against enemies of the Church.

THE BATTLING KNIGHT

But the Church was not always in control of the knights' activities. If there was an emergency, a military leader could use the old system and knight as many squires as he could afford to equip, with virtually no religious ceremony at all. He could even knight merchants and craftsmen from the towns if he needed more men in a hurry.

The training of knights, and young squires who had not yet reached the status of knight, concentrated on strength, fitness, individual skill with weapons, and, above all, the ability to fight as part of a team of disciplined armored horsemen.

Medieval horsemen used spurs to prick the sides of their horses when they wanted the animals to move faster. Gilded or decorated spurs became the most important badge of knightly rank. This late 14th-century example has a revolving spiked disc at the back.

This diagram shows how the feudal system was supposed to work. Each arrow shows the loyalty or service owed by one group of people to their feudal superiors. For example, knights were usually given estates by a baron or the Church and so owed loyalty to them. Even here the pattern is greatly simplified!

O nce a knight was accepted as a member of the aristocracy, he had to take on new duties. In fact the knight became the most important element in what is called the feudal system. He defended the peasants while they worked to feed him and the rest of society.

At least, that was the theory. In fact there never was one version of the feudal system. It varied from place to place, as well as from century to century. Some historians argue that the feudal system never really existed!

THE FEUDAL SYSTEM

The most typical feudal system in the 12th and 13th centuries was found in the countryside. There was a king at the top and peasants at the bottom, with knights somewhere in the middle.

A knight often lived in a castle or manor house on his estate, called a *fief*, pronounced "fee." This was a piece of land farmed by peasants who produced enough food and taxes to support the knight and his household. The knight gathered taxes, took his turn guarding a castle for the local baron, and might serve in his lord's army. Barons, in turn, governed large areas in the king's name—though they were often as powerful as the king himself.

PROBLEMS WITH THE SYSTEM

However, in some parts of Europe there was not enough land for all knights to have fiefs. Many were given money fiefs instead. These might be taxes collected on trade or tolls. In some places, knights lived in towns. Thus a knight might feel loyalty to the town and its merchants, as well as to the person who had given him the money fief.

A knight promised to be loyal to his lord or king and to do military service for him. In return the lord or king promised to protect the knight and usually gave him a fief to live on.

DIVIDED LOYALTIES

Many knights lived on lands owned by the Church. The Church and its bishops often felt that their first loyalty was to the Pope and to God, not to a king. Some other knights simply served as paid mercenaries for whoever offered the most money, which meant that they were outside the feudal system altogether. This led to more confusion and divided loyalties.

During the 11th century, the Church needed the support of law-abiding knights to impose the Peace of God. Below, knights help a priest arrest a knight or robber-baron who has been breaking the law. Only knights had the military power to stop other knights who ignored the law.

THE PEACE OF GOD

As a result, many powerful barons and knights believed that they were free to fight their own private wars. This brought chaos and fear to places such as southern France and Germany. Most of the kings were too weak to stop these wars. The Church tried to bring back law and order through the Peace of God movement. This insisted that private wars could only be fought on certain days of the week. Rulers also tried to impose rules dealing with who could fight and who could be attacked. Gradually, some order was restored, but some kings, barons, and knights continued to fight each other.

Knights did not only fight as heavily armored cavalry in battle. They also had to guard and defend castles, and command the sergeants and militias (local soldiers) in fortified towns. In return, local men, women, and children had their own duties, such as bringing food and water for the soldiers.

13

Destriers, specially bred war-horses, were very expensive so they were looked after carefully. Books were written on the subject. Some of them included advanced veterinary science translated from Arabic.

The knight's most important possession was his specially bred war-horse, the "destrier." Without this expensive animal, the knight could not be a full member of the cavalry elite. In training he practiced using weapons while riding this large animal, and fighting in a close-packed, highly disciplined cavalry formation. War-horses were looked after carefully and were so valuable that some wealthy knights even dressed them in armor before going to battle.

THE KNIGHT AND HIS HORSE

In battle, a closely packed group of knights on horseback walked into the attack, then lowered their lances to make their final charge at a slow canter. The sight of dozens of knights riding side by side, with the blades of their lances only a few feet apart, must have been a frightening one.

When charging, a knight almost stood in his stirrups (foot supports), but was held steady by the raised back of his tall, wood-framed saddle, which gripped his hips. He held his heavy lance, over twelve feet long, in the "couched" position, locked tight under the right armpit. This meant it could only be moved a little to the left or right when he aimed at his target, but it gave him a very firm grip on the lance. Basically, the knight, horse, and lance became an almost unstoppable "missile." It was very difficult for another knight, let alone a foot soldier, to knock a knight off his horse. But once unhorsed, it was difficult for the knight to get back on again.

Based on the early 14th-century English Luttrell Psalter, this picture shows Sir Geoffrey Luttrell and his war-horse, fully armored and with the Luttrell coat of arms displayed on their equipment. Sir Geoffrey is being given his helmet and shield by his wife and daughter. Their clothes show their own heraldry.

14

THE ARMY

Knights were the leaders and backbone of most western European armies. They were supported by the squires, who only fought in an emergency, and professional cavalry sergeants who were not members of the aristocracy. There were also professional infantry sergeants, including highly paid archers. The thousands of ordinary foot soldiers might include well-equipped men from towns, or peasants forced to leave their homes in the country, who had little or no training.

By the 12th and 13th century, Italian knights fought on foot more often than French and German knights. They also had some of the most advanced arms and armor. The Italian knights in this carving have coats of arms displayed on their helmets, their shields, and their horses' cloth coats.

BATTLE TACTICS

To win a battle, the knights of one army usually had to defeat the knights of the enemy army. The other soldiers tried to protect their own knights. One of the most important battle tactics was the conrois. This was a close formation of knights designed to charge at standing infantry or other cavalry, and was the "tank" of medieval warfare. Only a brave and disciplined enemy could resist a conrois of fully armored knights if it did hit its target.

However, unlike a modern tank, the conrois could only move forward. If it was attacked from the side or rear it was almost helpless. It was also difficult to turn or stop a conrois once it had started to charge, and it was even more difficult to bring the knights back together if they got split up. In fact the conrois had to deliver a knock-out blow—or its knights could soon be defeated.

THE BATTLE OF MARCHFELD

The Battle of Marchfeld in A.D. 1278 (shown below) was a typical clash between armored cavalry knights. The Bohemian knights fought their enemy, the Austrian and Hungarian knights, to a standstill. However, a force of Turkish horse-archers who were fighting with the Austrians were nimble enough to get around the right side of the Bohemian conrois formations. Shooting arrows from horseback, they caused havoc. With their knights defeated, the Bohemians lost the battle.

On the battlefield, powerful infantry crossbows and field fortifications such as rows of sharp stakes could stop an advancing conrois. These tactics enabled the armies of small Italian states (left) to defeat the knights of larger German forces (right).

Key for Battle of Marchfeld

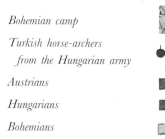

Bohemian camp

Turkish horse-archers from the Hungarian army

Austrians

Hungarians

Bohemians

MEDIEVAL CASTLES

The castle of Eltz is a typical example of the kind of hilltop fortification built in Germany. It is called a "randhausburgen," which means "surrounding-house-castle." Its position on a natural outcrop of rock made it difficult to attack.

Castles were the homes of kings, barons, and their knights, in addition to servants and other staff. Castles were also centers of local government as well as local defense. From them, law and order was maintained throughout the surrounding countryside.

MAGNIFICENCE AND SQUALOR

Castles looked very important, but they were actually uncomfortable to live in. There was little privacy for anyone, except for the lord and his lady, who had their own bedroom. Meals were eaten together, and there were only basic washing facilities. Despite the dirt and noise, life in a castle had a certain grandeur and was probably never boring.

LIFE IN THE CASTLE

It was part of a baron's or knight's duty to behave in a generous manner, entertaining guests, and giving work to other knights, servants, and laborers. Knights, squires, and sergeants of the castle would train in the courtyard, while armorers would be repairing weapons and armor in the outbuildings. Crops would be grown, taxes collected, and hunts organized both for military training and as an extra source of food. During a war, a strong garrison would be mounted on the walls, while scouts scoured the countryside for information.

Gates were the weakest points of any castle. Different systems were developed to strengthen them, including several ways of raising and lowering a drawbridge. The illustration below left shows a drawbridge protected by an iron gate called a portcullis and raised by a winch. Below right is a drawbridge balanced by heavy counterweights.

Counterweights

Portcullis

Feasts were held in the castle's hall. They were very carefully organized, with many different courses of food and drink. The more important guests sat closest to the high table where the lord and lady sat.

UNDER SIEGE

Castles usually had to be captured by a siege. At the first sign of an attack, the defenders made sure the castle had enough food, water, wine, and military supplies to last for months. They would also make sure the stores were filled with leather, nails, and iron to repair weapons or armor. Any wooden buildings near the outer walls would be destroyed, so the enemy could not use the timber. The castle's commander would also send messages to his lord asking for help.

ATTACK

Sometimes the defenders were able to attack the enemy before they could set up camp. If this failed, the defenders would retreat inside their fortifications. From there they might make sorties (attacks) to try to destroy the attackers' battering rams and food supplies.

HONORABLE SURRENDER

If a sortie failed, a castle's commander might enter into a temporary truce, agreeing to surrender if help had not arrived by an agreed date. In return, the attackers would agree not to harm the castle's defenders when they surrendered. However, defenders got little mercy if they had refused to submit when given the chance.

Only rarely would attackers try to take a castle by storm, because they risked losing too many soldiers. Instead, the attackers would try to starve the castle into submission, tunnel under the walls, or demolish the walls or gates with battering rams.

This manuscript shows the siege of Savona in Italy in 1227. Attackers and defenders both have stone-throwing "mangonels." These were basically enormous slings on beams powered by men and women pulling on ropes. Each side is trying to destroy the other's artillery. In the 12th century the counterweight mangonel, or "trebuchet," was invented in the Middle East. This used heavy weights instead of people pulling ropes.

17

HERALDRY AND STATUS

Warriors had painted designs on their shields and armor since well before the Middle Ages. What made the heraldry of medieval times special was that these symbolic designs, or insignia, began to be passed down from generation to generation. Men called heralds were employed by kings and military commanders to identify the insignia during tournaments and battles.

Direct relation →
Political claim ⟶
Political allegiance ⟶

This pommel from the grip of a sword has the coat of arms of Dreux on one side, and a typical French crusader's cross on the other. It was found in Damascus (now Syria) and was probably lost by Peter of Dreux, Count of Brittany, when he was captured by Egyptian Mamluks in A.D. 1250.

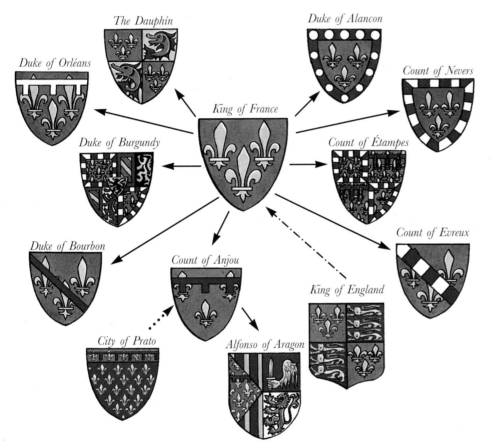

The Dauphin · Duke of Alancon · Duke of Orléans · Count of Nevers · King of France · Duke of Burgundy · Count of Étampes · Duke of Bourbon · Count of Anjou · King of England · Count of Evreux · City of Prato · Alfonso of Aragon

The relationships between different parts of the French royal family were shown in a pictorial way by heraldry. Marriage alliances and even political loyalty to France by foreigners could also be shown.

> Each strives to arm himself
> with a new clean surcoat.
> One has a tower shining
> brightly on his shield,
> one a lion, one a boar . . .
> This man bears a black banner,
> another white, another blue . . .
> another blazoned with
> a red coat covered with leaves.
>
> —— *From the poem "Galeran"* ——

WHY HERALDRY?

One reason heraldry emerged was because helmets began to have wider face protectors and chainmail hoods that covered most of the face, making it difficult to recognize the knight. Heraldry became a way of identifying an armored knight in battle or during a tournament.

THE USE OF HERALDRY

The origin of heraldry probably dates to the first crusades, when knights may have seen designs used by Arab and Byzantine soldiers, and brought the idea back to the West with them.

At first, only kings and members of the nobility used heraldic symbols, called "coats of arms." But gradually, knights and lesser nobilities adopted the use of coats of arms, creating variations on the traditional colors and symbols. A knight's family and political connections could be identified by "reading" his coat of arms.

Because few people in medieval times could read or write, a coat of arms might also be used as a "seal," an official stamp that was used as a sign of identity instead of a written signature.

FAMILY COATS OF ARMS

By the end of the twelfth century the basic rules of heraldry had developed. A fixed set of colors and a basic pattern were used by each noble family. This coat of arms was then inherited by a man's eldest son. His younger sons made theirs slightly different from the original, and their sons might add even more differences. Sometimes, husbands would add their wives' coat of arms to their own in a system called quartering, particularly if they had married into a powerful family.

Heraldry not only identified troops on the battlefield, but was also used to describe events in manuscripts. In the Italian chronicle below, the city-state of Florence is asking for help from the king of France. The city can be recognized because, like the blue and gold French banner, the Florentine flag includes a fleurs-de-lys.

BADGES OF LOYALTY

Families that had risen to the knightly class took pride in this fact by including something to do with their trade, such as business or farming, on their coats of arms. Towns did the same. For example, the coat of arms used by seaports included ships, while towns used crossed keys to show that their loyalty was—or had been—to the Pope.

In some parts of Europe, small states would also show their loyalty to a more powerful kingdom by adding part of its coat of arms to their own. In Italy, the little city of Prato and the powerful city of Florence used the French fleurs-de-lys to show loyalty to France.

One of the main reasons for the use of heraldry was the development of new forms of helmets that completely hid a knight's face so that he could not be recognized by friends or followers. This 13th-century bronze container called an "aquamanile" shows a knight wearing an early form of "Great Helm." The aquamanile could have held water or wine during a banquet.

COURTLY LOVE

Like all forms of hunting, falconry was used to get meat for eating. It was also a very aristocratic sport and was often associated with romantic flirting between men and women.

As knights changed from gruff, warfaring soldiers into true members of a new aristocracy, they started to take an interest in the finer things of life. Their knightly codes of honor—so important when facing an enemy on the battlefield—took on a different meaning back at home. Chivalry became the code of the day, with an emphasis on high moral standards and courtly behavior toward women.

TREATMENT OF WOMEN

In medieval Europe, the idea that men should treat women as anything other than possessions would have sounded crazy. But crusaders returning from the Middle East learned something from their Muslim adversaries, who revered the women in their society. Knightly behavior gradually evolved into a more civilized, even romantic code of conduct.

COURTLY LOVE

Knights and squires were encouraged to worship a woman and to perform heroic deeds in her name. She, in turn, would praise his bravery as far as was considered proper. This displeased leaders of the church, however, who feared such frivolous behavior would distract the knights from their higher purpose of serving the church.

CHIVALRY

The idea of courtly love soon became part of the ceremonies and customs of knighthood, in a code of conduct called chivalry. In addition to fighting for his lord and protecting the Church, a chivalrous knight was expected to be polite to women, to defend the weak, and to be truthful and honorable.

Minstrels and music sometimes played a part in the knighting ceremony. The young Francis of Assisi is given the sword and spurs that mark his promotion to the status of knight, while minstrels play a form of lute and doubled flute.

LADIES AND MINSTRELS

The ideals of courtly love were spread by traveling singers called minstrels. They sang new love songs played on unusual musical instruments from the Middle East.

The songs were so popular that even the Church grudgingly changed its opinion, especially since some of the best songs were being written by monks and nuns.

NEW INSTRUMENTS

The minstrels of the 12th to 14th centuries had different names in different countries, but they all sang similar songs. In France they were called "troubadours" and in Germany "minnesingers."

Their music changed over the years. At first it was played on simple instruments, like flutes and drums. Then travelers brought new ones from the East, such as the lute (similar to an Arabic instrument called an oud) or the viol (which was played with a bow and seems to have been brought from China by the Turks).

AN INTEREST IN ART

Quite suddenly it seemed that an almost barbaric western Europe was becoming interested in things other than warfare. In more peaceful areas, like England, many knights moved from being full-time warriors to being country gentlemen. They took more interest in governing their peasants, and in agriculture and business, than in military training. In places like France, Germany, and Italy, some knights and squires won fame as troubadours.

PATRONS

Once the ideals of chivalry had caught on, they encouraged an interest in art. The wealthier knights and nobles became patrons. Instead of using their wealth to build castles and fight wars, they began to pay artists, writers, poets, craftspeople, and academics to work for them. Many great religious works of art were paid for by knights and nobles.

The lute became a favorite instrument with minstrels. Its name comes from the Arabic "al-oud" which simply meant "the oud."

As the knightly class got richer and life became more comfortable, young squires were often criticized for spending too much time on the latest troubadour songs and not working hard enough at their military training.

21

Medieval tournaments were originally a form of military training for cavalrymen. They helped a knight refresh the skills needed to control a horse and use his weapons. Tournaments became the most popular spectator sport of the Middle Ages. Some knights traveled all over Europe to display their skills. However, by the 15th century these elaborate events had almost nothing to do with real warfare. They were a way of winning fame and fortune, because the winner often took the loser's horse or even his armor.

The training of Charlemagne's cavalrymen was basically the same as that of the Roman cavalry. It involved teams taking turns throwing blunt javelins at each other, the other side defending themselves with their shields.

ORIGINS OF THE TOURNAMENT

When Charlemagne and his successors built up their armies in the eighth and ninth centuries, they used some complicated forms of training based on the methods of the old Roman and Persian armies. For example, teams of horsemen armed with javelins took turns charging at each other. They would throw their blunted weapons, then turn away as a unit while the other team defended themselves with their shields.

By the 11th century, rival teams of knights were challenging each other apparently for sport. These matches gradually evolved into full-scale competitions called tournaments, organized by leading kings and barons.

By the 15th century, tournaments were an important spectator sport. The spectators the young knights really wanted to impress were young ladies, as this Italian wall painting of a joust makes very clear. The men on the ground are probably clearing up pieces of broken weapons.

THE MELÉE

The first sort of tournament was a mock battle that had more in common with real cavalry training than it did a spectator sport. Two teams of knights, normally in close-packed conrois formations, charged at each other. Then, when their formations had fallen apart, they mixed up in a general free-for-all, called a melée. It was not as chaotic as it sounds, because there were judges who would disqualify a knight for making an unfair blow, or would try to separate the teams if things got out of hand. Some melées also involved units of foot soldiers who would try to help their own knights.

During the skirmish a French squire from Beauce came forward alone and cried out, "Is there any gentleman among you who, for love of his lady, is willing to try a feat of arms with me? If there is one I am quite ready to ride forward, fully armed and mounted, to tilt three courses with the lance, to give three blows with the battle-axe, and three strokes with the dagger.". . . When his proposal was made known . . . an expert man at tournaments stepped forward and said, "I will accept his challenge; let him come out of the castle."

The Froissart Chronicles

JOUSTING

Jousting, in which two individual horsemen charged at each other, probably began as a way of settling disputes, letting off steam, or simply warming up. It reached the height of its popularity in the 13th century. Not only was jousting more entertaining for the audience, who could cheer on their own favorite, it also allowed a knight to show off his personal bravery and skill.

All forms of early tournament were very dangerous. As many knights seem to have been killed in tournaments as died in battle. Later, rules were introduced to make tournaments safer for the contestants. For example, a knight had to hit his opponent's shield or helmet; hitting his legs or horse was counted as a foul.

A COLORFUL SPORT

By the 15th century, tournaments were not any more dangerous than modern sports, though a lot more colorful. Nevertheless, knights could also still challenge opponents to a dangerous fight with real war-weapons rather than with blunt blades.

Images of the tournament were often used to illustrate romantic stories. Here knights are not fighting each other but are besieging a "Castle of Love" that is guarded by ladies who defend themselves by throwing flowers at the "enemy."

In this Italian wall-painting, Geoffrey de Bouillon, the first ruler of the kingdom of Jerusalem, is armed for tournament combat on foot, in the style of the late 15th century. The female figure is carrying a kind of pickax used in duels to settle legal arguments.

The outbuildings of the manor house were full of activity, including cider-making. The inset, far right, shows a special barrel-shaped cider-press. This crushes the apples, then the juice is strained through a cloth before being put in barrels to brew. The only brick or stone structure in many manor houses was the chimney; the rest was made of timber and plaster. Even with a roaring fire, the lord and lady's chamber (shown when the see-through scene is turned) was probably chilly. But it was still more comfortable than a castle!

As early as the 13th century, many English knights were turning away from their warlike way of life to something more stable. Compared with most other parts of Europe, England at this time was a peaceful place. As a result, the knightly class gradually changed from professional soldiers to "village squires," the leaders of society in the rural areas. They began to be more concerned with governing the peasants, selling the wool from their sheep, and keeping local law and order, than fighting the king's enemies in foreign lands.

THE PEACEFUL KNIGHT

By the late 14th century many English knights lived in comfortable manor houses rather than cold and drafty castles. Of course, the manor houses still had to be defended, since England still had outlaws, pirates, political disturbances, uprisings in Wales, and invasions by the Scots or the French.

The manor house shown below is based on some buildings and deserted moats that can still be seen in the English countryside. The defenses consist of a wooden stockade and drawbridge. Inside this stockade is the main house and some outbuildings consisting of stables and a brewery where servants are making cider.

EVERYDAY LIFE

Much of the everyday life and work of the manor house takes place outside in the courtyard. In the scene below, boys on a wheeled wooden hobby-horse are tilting at a quintain, while young men are practicing sword-play. There are some armorers mending weapons and shields, perhaps because there are problems with outlaws. Meanwhile, some peasants are taking a cart loaded with cider to sell at the local market.

INSIDE THE HOUSE

Inside the main house, the knight's family dine in the main hall. The other downstairs rooms are used for storage and work, including the kitchen and the buttery for storing barrels of wine, beer, or salted food. Only the lord of the manor and his close family have any privacy. At night they will sleep in the only bedroom on the first floor. But as it is now daytime, this is where women spin, bathe the children, and carry out other household chores.

THE VILLAGE

Beyond the moat is a small chapel. Also close to the manor house is a village. The villagers look to the knight and his family for protection, and also for advice.

When you turn the see-through scene, can you see the smoke from a distant warning beacon? This is a signal for the local forces to assemble, led by the local knight. The knight's duties also included keeping law and order in the surrounding villages, and serving as a link with the king's government.

1 Chapel
2 Moat
3 Drawbridge
4 Stockade
5 Stable
6 Brewery
7 Great hall
8 Kitchen
9 Lord and lady's bedroom

Knights usually wanted to appear in armor on their tombs, even if they were really peaceful country gentlemen. The incised brass carving (above) marked the tomb of Sir John de la Pole and his wife. Sir John is shown in full armor of the late 14th century.

PILGRIMAGE

Pilgrim routes crisscrossed Europe and the Mediterranean. The most important centers of pilgrimage were Jerusalem, Rome, Santiago de Compostela in Spain, and Canterbury. Other important centers of pilgrimage attracted local visitors.

Most medieval people were deeply religious. They believed that doing penance (something to show you are sorry for your sins) or making some sort of sacrifice could wash their sins away and save their souls from hell. One of the most important forms of penance was to go on pilgrimage (visit a holy place).

SAVING THE SOUL

Pilgrimage to Christian sites was extremely important during the Middle Ages. Poor people, including lower-ranking knights, visited the tombs of local saints, since only the rich could afford to travel far. It cost a lot of money to reach one of the major Christian centers, such as Rome or Jerusalem. If pilgrims were not rich, they would only be able to go as part of the staff of a great lord.

- ● Main pilgrim centers
- ● Other pilgrim centers

NORTH SEA

Canterbury

BLACK SEA

Santiago de Compostela

Jerusalem

Rome

MEDITERRANEAN SEA

Going on pilgrimage was a hazardous undertaking. The main dangers were disease, shipwreck, and attack by robbers. Even in peacetime, groups of pilgrims might need a knight to travel with them for protection. In the Holy Land, this would probably be a Hospitaller or Knight Templar.

Almost every country in Christendom had its own pilgrimage centers, but the most important was the Holy Sepulcher in Jerusalem. Christian pilgrims made their way there before the crusades, and they continued to do so after the West lost its hold on Jerusalem.

DANGER ON THE ROAD

Traveling was hard and dangerous. Many people were attacked by bandits and outlaws. Roads were bad, there were no hotels, and inns were crude shelters. Instead, people tried to rest at monasteries, or at one of the special hostels run for pilgrims by monks or friars along the main pilgrim routes.

KNIGHTS ON PILGRIMAGE

The Church encouraged knights to go on pilgrimage so they could protect other pilgrims from bandits and outlaws. The knights and their families responded enthusiastically, because they were often adventurous by nature. Perhaps knights also believed their souls needed saving because their job involved such violence and bloodshed. Knights who had very guilty consciences could either give up all their worldly goods and family to join one of the military orders that served the church, or volunteer to fight alongside the orders for just one season.

RELIGIOUS TOURISM

However, as traveling conditions improved during the late Middle Ages, knights, merchants, rich peasants, and strong-minded women went on pilgrimage for reasons other than penance. Many were more like modern tourists than the serious pilgrims of earlier centuries. They even collected souvenirs, lead badges with the symbols of the saint or religious event linked with the place they had visited.

Those who wanted real adventure now had to go further, to the Holy Land in the Middle East, which had been reconquered by the Muslims.

One of the most popular pilgrim badges in England was "Thomas Becket's Flask." This miniature lead container was supposed to contain the saint's diluted blood, which was believed to work miraculous cures on the sick.

Not all centers of pilgrimage were simply religious. Some were famous because they contained the tombs of great rulers, such as Charlemagne, who was regarded almost as a saint in the Middle Ages. This golden reliquary, containing his bones, portrayed him as Sanctus Karolus Imperator, builder of a new and Christian Roman Empire, a man blessed by God and supported by the Church.

THE CRUSADES

The Byzantine Empire was the eastern half of the old Roman Empire. In the late 11th century, the Seljuk Turks overran half of the Byzantine Empire. In desperation the emperor begged for help from the West. He wanted trained mercenaries to join his armies in Constantinople—instead he got a crusade!

DEUS VULT

The First Crusade to reconquer the Holy Land was called by Pope Urban II in A.D. 1095. Although Jerusalem had already been ruled by Muslims for over 400 years, the Seljuk Turks had begun making it difficult for pilgrims to visit the Holy Land. The crusade was sent to take back Jerusalem and uphold Christianity.

The Pope probably did not expect his call to reclaim Jerusalem to be so popular. In 1096, over 5,000 knights "took up the cross" and marched east with *Deus Vult*— "It is God's Will"—as their battle cry. Thousands of ordinary people did the same. In all, about 150,000 men, women and children became crusaders.

Western European warriors were recruited by the Byzantine Empire long before the crusades. They included Normans, as well as Anglo-Saxons who had fled from England after the Norman Conquest—so quarrels were probably quite common.

The citadel of Amasya, in Turkey, includes a great deal of medieval Byzantine fortification. The tower shaped like the prow of a ship, on the left, is typically Byzantine. The citadel was an important military base used to defeat a Christian crusade in A.D. 1101.

Main Crusade Routes

First ---------   Fourth ---------

Second -·-·-·-   Fifth ·········

Third +-+-+-+   St Louis ++++++++
of France

BLACK SEA

Paris

Venice

Constantinople

Antioch

Rome

Messina

Jerusalem

THE CAPTURE OF JERUSALEM

The Middle Eastern crusades are seen as important events in European history since they were an international effort to take back the Holy Land from Muslim rule. In fact, the First Crusade was the only successful one. It conquered Palestine, most of Lebanon, part of Jordan, and part of Syria. In 1099, a force of just 1,000 knights and 10,000 footsoldiers managed to capture Jerusalem, and set up a number of crusader states.

Like later crusades, the First Crusade was marked by great cruelty and suffering. Few of the knights knew anything about the land and its difficult climate, and many were killed by thirst, hunger, and disease rather than by their enemies. The crusaders also killed thousands of Muslims when they captured Jerusalem.

LATER CRUSADES

Later crusades involved knights and other professional soldiers who were generally better organized and equipped than those who fought in the First Crusade. For almost 200 years, the crusaders managed to defend part of what had already been won.

WHY THE CRUSADES FAILED

However, crusades that tried to take more land almost always failed, despite involving some of the very best armies of knights that Europe could gather. Such disasters puzzled the knights and churchmen. The churchmen were convinced God was on their side and the knights were sure they were the best fighting men in the world. The success of the First Crusade was really a fluke, because it had hit the Muslim Middle East at a time of great weakness. Once the Muslim armies got over the first shock, they quickly learned how to deal with the crusaders' tactics.

THE THIRD CRUSADE

By the time the Third Crusade reached the Holy Land, Richard the Lionheart of England, Philip of France, and Frederick Barbarossa of Germany found themselves up against the great Saracen ruler Saladin, who was now in control of Jerusalem. The knights, sergeants, and other troops of England, France, and the German Empire did their best but could not even reach Jerusalem, let alone retake it from Saladin's soldiers.

Experience fighting the Muslims, Mongols, and Byzantines taught Western knights a great deal and encouraged the development of new forms of arms and armor. The so-called "dog-face basinet" with its chainmail neck protection (below) is an example of how European armorers learned from the East and then added their own ideas.

FIGHTING FOR THE CROSS

The success of the First Crusade was never repeated. This late 13th-century manuscript shows the crusaders' desperate but eventually successful attack on the city of Antioch.

Most of the crusades to the Holy Land failed, though the crusaders did hang on to some parts of the eastern Mediterranean coast until the late 13th century, as well as the island of Cyprus. The Fourth Crusade even attacked the Byzantine Empire and occupied Constantinople for more than 50 years!

CRUSADING AMID THE SNOWS

Other, later crusades tried to stop the Ottoman Turks from destroying what was left of the Byzantine Empire, and conquering the Balkans, part of central Europe and southern Russia. They failed as well. In fact, for the knights of western Europe the crusades were a heroic disaster. In man-to-man combat with their enemies, the heavily armored knights were almost unbeatable. Yet tactically they were not as clever as the Muslims. The relatively small crusader armies could never really hope to defeat Turkish and Arab forces who were defending their homes and land.

Far to the north, German knights led a series of crusades against the pagan peoples of what are now northeast Germany, northern Poland, and the Baltic states. They were much more successful. Here, knights, sergeants, and warlike priests forced Christianity upon the citizens at the point of a sword. These campaigns were very ruthless, and in the 14th century Lithuania, the last pagan state in Europe, finally accepted Christianity.

The First Crusade of 1096–1100 suffered terrible hardship as it marched across Europe and Turkey. Unused to the land and climate, many died from hunger, thirst, and disease. When the crusaders reached Jerusalem, many knights and ordinary soldiers lost control, slaughtering not only Muslim soldiers, but women and children.

Conrad, a well-armored knight and riding an armored horse, attacked the Lithuanians with only a few Germans. But God sent such fear into the hearts of the Lithuanians, and they were so dazzled by the Germans' shining weapons, that they fled in all directions.

The Livonian Rhymed Chronicle

SPAIN AND PORTUGAL

Things were also different in Spain and Portugal. Here the Christians outnumbered the Muslims and were much closer to their own lands. The campaigns in Spain and Portugal were known as the "Reconquista" rather than crusades, and they steadily pushed the Christian frontier southward, from one chain of mountains, called sierras, to the next. Eventually the Spanish and Portuguese knights, helped by volunteers from north of the Pyrenees, retook Andalusia from the Muslims and even tried to attack North Africa. The greatest of the Spanish knights was Rodrigo de Vivar, "El Cid," meaning "the master" in Arabic.

PEASANT CAVALRY

In most of Europe the armored horsemen were knights or squires, or at least professional soldiers. In Spain they were aided by ordinary villagers and townsmen who formed large mounted militia forces. These fought in almost exactly the same way as their noble knightly neighbors.

The Baltic crusades are less well known than those to the Middle East. But they also had their epic triumphs and disasters. One of the most famous defeats was on the frontier between Estonia and Russia, in 1242. On the frozen surface of Lake Peipus, an entire force of Teutonic knights is said to have fallen through the ice.

These two figures are from a letter of loyalty sent by the Italian town of Prato to the King of Naples, who was related to the Count of Anjou. The well equipped soldier on the left holds a shield that includes the royal coat of arms. The other knight's shield has the Latin word "LEX" (meaning "law") to show that Prato's loyalty was confirmed by law.

31

THE SIEGE AT AIN HABIS

The crusaders, like their Saracen enemies, built some huge and elaborate castles. They also used whatever they found when they needed a fortification in a hurry. These included ancient Roman theaters and temples, and caves in the mountains. One of the most famous cave fortresses was Ain Habis, or the "Caves de Sueth."

A CAVE FORTRESS

Long before the crusaders arrived, one of the vertical cliffs overlooking the deep Yarmouk river valley was home to some Byzantine monks. Nobody knows when these monks left their isolated monastery.

A READY-MADE FORTRESS

The crusaders did not have enough time, money, or manpower to build a full-scale castle, so they took over the caves that the monks had cut into the cliff-face and linked by wooden walkways. From Ain Habis, the crusaders could threaten the vital road that linked Damascus and other great cities of Syria with Arabia and Egypt.

Ain Habis may have housed only a small crusader garrison, but its position was so vital that the Saracens were determined to get it back.

1. Muslim troops have broken through the stone gate
2. Old Byzantine monks' church
3. Saracen miners cut a steep passage to upper level
4. Wooden walkways joining sets of caves
5. Ladders between levels
6. Waterfall
7. Troughs channeling water into main cistern
8. Main water storage cistern
9. Crusader garrison defending upper caves and walkways
10. Upper living quarters including second church

BATTLES FOR THE CAVES

But besieging a series of caves in a cliff was not like attacking an ordinary castle. The first assault, in 1158, was abandoned because the main Saracen army was defeated elsewhere. However, it convinced King Baldwin III of Jerusalem to send supplies and a bigger garrison to Ain Habis.

THE SARACENS SUCCEED

In 1182, the great Muslim ruler Saladin sent his nephew Farrukh Shah to attack again. This time the cave fortress fell after only five days. The attack is shown in the scene below, with Muslim miners digging a steep passage from next to a cave-church to one of the main storerooms above.

The crusaders retook the caves later that same year. Miners cut boulders from the top of the cliff and sent them crashing onto the wooden walkways, smashing the water troughs. Without water, the Muslim garrison could not survive.

The crusaders brought many stonemasons and put them on top of the mountains, placing a strong guard of horsemen and sergeants so they could work in safety day and night. They threw the rocks they excavated over the cliff (onto the defenders below).

—— *William of Tyre* ——

WOUNDS AND MEDICINE

The terrible injuries inflicted by medieval weapons were often shown in gruesome detail in medieval manuscripts. This scene from a 13th-century Bible shows Hebrews defeating the Amonnites.

HORRORS OF WAR

Death from accidents or disease was so common during medieval times that people were probably more able to accept the sight of blood and the gruesome reality of war. They also seemed able to survive appalling wounds, despite the crude medical facilities of the time. Perhaps by surviving daily in the unhygienic world around them, children and adults were more resistant to infection.

Descriptions of battles in medieval books say that the most common injuries were to the extremities—the arms, legs, and head. This was because a knight's body was largely protected by his armor and a shield. Studies of medieval battle skeletons have found this to be true.

Like soldiers in any period of history, knights faced the risk of being injured or killed. Medieval weapons might look basic, but they could cut off an arm, leg, or head with a single blow, while arrows sometimes really did fall like rain.

Because of the superiority of Islamic medical science, Muslim soldiers regarded the crusaders as dirty and ignorant. It took a long time for European knights to accept that hot baths were good for you, rather than a luxury for soft Saracens. Baths were even found in Muslim military camps, shown below. The hot water was supplied from steaming cauldrons.

Discovered in a mass grave from the Battle of Visby, 1361, the skull above was almost cut in half by a terrible blow across the front despite the fact that the wearer had a chainmail coif. Meanwhile, Middle Eastern doctors had already discovered how blood circulated through the body (shown below), and how the eyes worked—information not believed in western Europe for centuries.

MEDICAL KNOWLEDGE

In the early Middle Ages, there were no doctors in the armies of western Europe. Instead priests did what they could, though this usually only meant giving words of comfort to the dying.

Ancient Greek medical knowledge did not survive in Europe, but was translated into Arabic by the Muslims. Arab and Persian doctors had discovered even more about how the body worked. By the 11th and 12th centuries the crusaders had a chance to see just how advanced their Muslim and Byzantine rivals were in the fields of medical and veterinary science.

MIDDLE EASTERN SUPERIORITY

For example, in the 12th century, a Saracen soldier, Usamah Ibn Munqidh, wrote about a European and an Arab doctor. A knight with an infected leg was brought to the Arab doctor who put a small poultice (medicated bandage) on it. The infection began to heal, but then the European doctor came along and said, "This man knows nothing." He turned to the knight and asked, "What would you prefer, living with one leg or dying with two?" The knight replied, "Living with one leg." So the European doctor called for a strong soldier with a sharp ax. He put the knight's leg on a block of wood and told the soldier to cut it off with a single blow. This the soldier tried to do, but it needed two blows, at which point the patient died. The Arab doctor was not impressed; nor was Usamah.

LEARNING ON THE BATTLEFIELD

During the 13th and 14th centuries, the medical and veterinary knowledge of the Middle East was brought to Europe via the crusaders and translated into Italian and Spanish. This meant that the science of medicine improved in many parts of Europe by the 15th century.

However, the Church was opposed to cutting up human bodies to study them, so a battle was sometimes a doctor's only chance to study the human body. Some doctors clearly knew what they were doing, because they also helped some people at the same time. For example, at the Battle of Fornovo in 1495, a wounded knight had several pieces of broken bone removed from his skull and was walking around the streets of Venice only a few weeks later.

No one knows why the Crusading Military Orders evolved in Spain and the Holy Land during the 12th century. Some historians believe they were inspired by the "ribats" where Muslims volunteered to pray and fight for their religion. Some orders only lasted a short time; others still exist today, though as charitable organizations rather than armies of knights.

A SWORD FOR THE CHURCH

Knights who wanted to lead a religious life but found it difficult to give up fighting could join one of the military orders. Unlike monks who stayed within the walls of their monasteries and prayed, members of a military order fought for the Church and could be sent anywhere. They became known as Knights of the Cross.

Knight Hospitallers tend the sick in an early hospital. This order started out with the mission of caring for sick pilgrims in the Holy Land. But they soon took on the duty of protecting pilgrims as well and so became one of the fighting orders.

Member of the Crusading Military Orders promised to give up all worldly possessions and, like monks, took a vow of poverty. For the Templar, the image of two knights riding a single horse reflects this poverty, though of course they did not really ride this way.

I . . . do profess and promise chastity, giving up all property, and obedience to God and to the Blessed Virgin Mary and to you, Brother . . . Master of the Teutonic Order, and to your successors, according to the Rules and Regulations of the Order. And I will be obedient to you, and to your successors, even unto death.

———— Brother-knights' Oath ————

MILITARY ORDERS

The most famous and successful of the military orders were the Templar, the Hospitallers, and the Teutonic Knights, all of which were created in the 12th century. They became the shock troops of the crusades and many other wars against non-Christians. In fact the military orders were so feared by their enemies that they were usually killed rather than taken prisoner. The cross of the order was clearly visible on the clothes they wore.

BROTHER-KNIGHTS

Military orders, such as the Templar, Hospitallers, Teutonic Knights, and others, also attracted large numbers of ordinary knights who then became "brother-knights." Volunteers who were not knights served as sergeants or as nonmilitary servants. Whatever their status, they gave up family, wealth, and position in return for a hard and precarious life, serving under very strict discipline and often in the most dangerous conditions.

Knights who did not want to dedicate themselves completely to the military orders became short-term members, serving in the orders' armies for a year or even for just one campaign. They could then go home feeling they had fought for God, perhaps earned a place in heaven, and also become heroes in the eyes of their friends.

The Templar church of Vera Cruz in Segovia, Spain. Many churches built for the Order of Templar were round, based on the Dome of the Rock in Jerusalem, which was thought to be the ancient temple where Jesus was shown to the priests. In fact it was a Muslim shrine built at the end of the seventh century.

A DANGEROUS LIFE

Brother-knights in the crusader states, the Baltic, or other warlike areas attacked their enemies, defended Christian territory against enemy raids, and kept up a rigorous daily training program. They were supported by brother-knights based all over Europe who gathered money and supplies, and then sent them to the men on the front line. As a result, the military orders soon became like powerful and rich international business corporations. They could even influence emperors and Popes.

MILITARY ORDERS AS RULERS

The Hospitallers and Teutonic Knights both ended up having their own states, the Hospitallers on the island of Rhodes, and later on Malta, while the Teutonic Knights ruled much of what is now northern Poland, Latvia, and Estonia.

The Templar, however, became so rich and powerful that the Pope and the king of France considered them a threat. The French king also hoped to take over their wealth. The Templar leadership was accused of spreading un-Christian beliefs. Confessions were forced out by torture, and the leaders were executed. The Order's ordinary members were given lesser punishments or were dismissed. Ironically, within months, the French king and the Pope were dead—just as one executed Templar leader had predicted!

Montfort, in northern Palestine, was the most important castle held by the German Military Order of Teutonic Knights in the Kingdom of Jerusalem. The Germans called it the Starkenberg which, like Montfort in French, means "strong mountain." Today it is in ruins, but the huge water cisterns that enabled its garrison to withstand a long siege still exist beneath the tumbled walls.

After the crusades, the Knights Templar fought very few battles. In the 14th century, they were accused of not following the Christian faith and their leaders were tortured and then burned.

INVASION FROM THE EAST

This helmet of the Russian Prince Yaroslav Vsevolodovic (below) was found under a bush centuries after it was lost in battle. The silver icon (religious picture) on the front proclaimed that Yaroslav was a Christian ruler, and was also believed to give its wearer extra protection.

In the **13th century**, a completely **new enemy suddenly burst into eastern and central Europe—the Mongols. They seemed to appear from nowhere and fought in a way that Russian warriors and European knights found almost impossible to deal with.**

THE MONGOLS

The Mongols were nomads from the plains to the east of Russia. They were tough warriors who rode fast horses and fought in the traditional Turkish manner as horse-archers. They had also learned a great deal from their Chinese enemies far to the east. A Mongol warrior could shoot his powerful bow from his saddle, and also carried a lance or sword. United under one ruthless ruler, the Great Khan Genghis, their military discipline astonished the European knights.

Most fortifications in medieval Russia, along with almost all other buildings, were made of wood. The only stone buildings were a few important churches. This kind of timber and earth defense was very strong, but even so it could not withstand the Mongol onslaught.

This early 14th-century manuscript from Iran shows the Mongols' different kinds of armor and powerful bows very accurately, along with the great war-drums they used as a way of communicating in battle.

THE MONGOLS ATTACK RUSSIA

First, the Mongols invaded Russia, taking their enemies completely by surprise. In winter their armies marched up the frozen rivers, using them as highways deep into the heart of Russia, so that the major cities fell within three years.

MONGOL VICTORY

Next, in 1241, the Mongols invaded central Europe. They astounded people with their ruthlessness and the speed at which their forces crossed great distances in almost all weathers. No wonder the knights of Europe called them "The Devil's Horsemen."

At the Battle of Liegnitz in Poland, the Mongols showered their enemies with arrows, then pretended to retreat. This lured the Teutonic Knights away from their army, so the Mongols could turn and crush them. Then, at the Sajo River, the Mongols used surprise attacks, smoke, and noise to confuse a larger Hungarian army, which panicked and fled.

WHY DID THE MONGOLS STOP?

The Mongols abruptly stopped their invasion of Europe, even though they had not been defeated. It seemed that they had just decided to go home. Many Christians believed this was "Divine intervention" (an act of God). The Great Khan had died, so his generals had gone to Mongolia to choose a successor and protect themselves against rivals.

The Mongols never returned to Europe to continue their invasion because they were not interested in taking over what they considered to be a poor and backward part of the world.

The Mongols were successful partly because they were willing to recruit soldiers from people they had conquered. This early 14th-century illustration shows Mongol troops, including a Middle Eastern Muslim Arab operating a stone-throwing "trebuchet."

The Mongol horse-archers appeared indestructible, faster, and more mobile than Western European knights. They also used fearsome new Chinese weapons—including early forms of gunpowder.

KNIGHTS AFLOAT

*Many medieval ports were
surrounded by defensive walls,
with towers overlooking their
narrow entrance. The entrance
could be blocked by a floating
boom or a chain raised and
lowered with a winch, shown on
the right-hand page. The tower
would have contained a small
mangonel similar to the one
shown top right. Within the
safety of this inner harbor, ships
were built, repaired, loaded, and
unloaded. When the see-through
page is turned, we can see the
left-hand tarida being loaded
with the knight's horses and
armor ready for battle, while the
right-hand merchant ship holds
knights and supplies.*

In some parts of medieval
Europe, knights were as likely
to find themselves serving
aboard ship as in an army on
land. Knights used lighter armor
and weapons aboard ship than
when riding a destrier.

THE KNIGHT AS MARINE

The Italian merchant states of Venice
and Genoa were the most powerful naval
forces of the Middle Ages. Their knights
played the part of marines defending
merchant ships and war-galleys. Rivals
joked that Venetian knights had webbed

feet and did not know how to ride
properly! However, northern Italian armies
often defeated large and powerful German
and French armies. At sea, the knights
and their crossbowmen were able to defeat
anyone that got in their way.

MEDIEVAL FIGHTING SHIPS

The main medieval fighting ship was the
galley. This used sails when cruising
peacefully and relied on oars during battle.
The oarsmen were not slaves, but free
men paid by the shipowners. The ship's
"sailors" were a small and highly skilled
group of men who handled the sails.

THE TARIDA

The Tarida was a specialized galley invented by Muslim Arabs to carry war-horses on raids overseas. It was larger and slower than a fighting galley but could carry less cargo than a merchant ship. Taridas were able to land men and horses, including fully armored knights, right on an enemy beach. They could also defend themselves if attacked at sea. Galleys, taridas, and merchant ships brought men, horses, and food to the crusaders in the Holy Land.

1 **Merchant ship or "round ship"**
2 **Chain across harbor mouth**
3 **Winch to raise or lower chain**
4 **Tarida**
5 **Loading door, sealed with pitch during the voyage**
6 **Horses in canvas cradles to support them during the voyage**
7 **Oarsmen (all free men, not slaves)**

NAVAL BATTLES

Naval fights usually started by shooting bows and crossbows from a distance, in an attempt to wound the enemy crew. A captain would try to get his ship alongside the enemy ship, so that the knights and soldiers who formed his fighting marines could rush across and try to capture the enemy vessel and its cargo intact.

A merchant ship is attacked by two sleek galleys on this 13th-century painted panel from Catalonia. All the ships carry armored knights.

URBAN KNIGHTS

After the crusader states in the Middle East lost most of their territory to the Muslims, they were left with only the seaports and a narrow strip of land on the coast. Most knights now lived in these coastal cities and so they had to rely on money fiefs. These included sugar cane factories (below) that were often worked by Muslim slaves whose only chance of escape was to convert to Christianity.

Some knights had always lived in towns, particularly in southern Europe. In Italy these urban knights were a major political as well as military force. Knights commanded most city militias, but they also dominated many town councils—at least until the merchant class grew rich enough to challenge the knights' power. Other knightly families went into war as a business; they hired themselves and their followers out as ready-made armies to whoever paid the most.

MONEY FIEFS

Many kings and barons did not have enough land to give all their knights fiefs or estates, so those who were rich enough offered "money fiefs" instead. Basically these were just a way in which a knight could raise the cash he needed to live and to pay for his expensive arms, armor, war-horse, and servants. Money fiefs might be taxes on a weekly market, tolls collected for the use of a bridge or ferry, or money made from a factory or other business. Knights who lived in towns or cities were, of course, more likely to have money fiefs than knights who lived in the countryside.

MERCHANT KNIGHTS

Experience in naval warfare and military service overseas could also be useful for a knight thinking of earning extra money as a part-time merchant. Some even worked in the slave trade (see quotation next page) that flourished in parts of Europe.

At the same time, many rich merchant families bought themselves aristocratic status by lending money to a ruler who could make them into knights but who happened to be short of money. In Italy, these knights often lived in fortified houses in rich merchant cities rather than castles.

THE BUSINESS OF WAR

The most obvious business for any knight, whether he lived in a town or the countryside, was the mercenary business, fighting for whoever would pay him. By the 14th century many rich cities, particularly in Italy, were run by merchants who preferred to hire ready-made armies rather than rely on local militias or have to fight as soldiers themselves. Successful mercenary leaders employed their own knights, squires, and infantrymen to make up a "company."

COMPANY WARFARE

When one war was over, a mercenary company would either split up or march off in search of another conflict and another employer.

For example, the Catalan Great Company consisted of experienced Spanish warriors who hired themselves out to the Byzantine emperor following the end of a war in southern Italy. Eventually they carved out their own small state around Athens in Greece—a state that survived to the end of the Middle Ages.

Knights fought at sea as well as on land. Spanish and Italian knights were particularly skilled in warfare at sea, manning fleets of war-galleys, serving as marines aboard rich trading ships, and turning to piracy when all else failed.

THE WHITE COMPANY

The most famous company in 14th century Italy was the White Company led by Sir John Hawkwood, an English knight who learned his business fighting the French during the Hundred Years War. In fact the later battles of the Hundred Years' War were not between Englishmen and Frenchmen fighting for their countries, but tough professionals who were more interested in keeping a profitable war going than in winning a final victory!

The rich merchant cities of Italy had their own urban knights, who lived in fortified houses rather than castles. Some owned tall torre (towers) inside the city walls. There were so many of these torre that some Italian cities, such as the little town of San Gimignano (above), were compared to forests.

The knights kept law and order within the city. However knights with different loyalties sometimes ended up fighting each other (below).

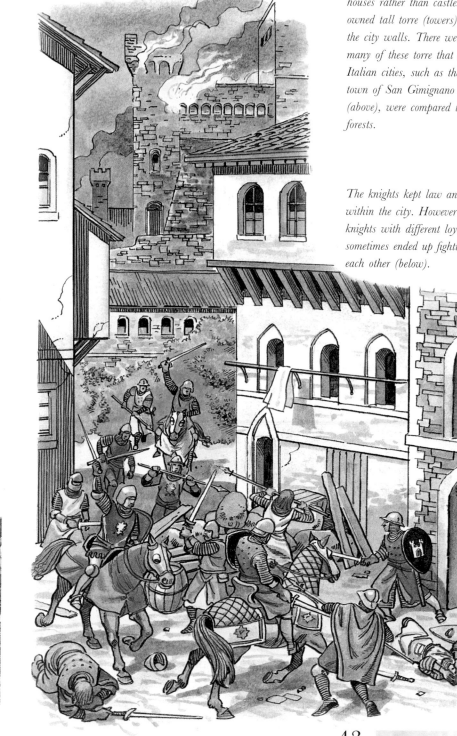

DECLINE OF THE KNIGHT

FULL-TIME SOLDIERS

By the 15th century, kings still needed soldiers who were full-time professionals. In nearly all countries the law still said that rulers could demand military service from their knights. But now many knights were country gentlemen, courtiers, or government officials.

So what was the point of demanding military service when most knights were neither trained as soldiers nor interested in fighting? From a king's point of view it made much more sense to hire professional mercenaries who would fight at any time of the year.

Most of the earliest illustrations of firearms do not look at all realistic. But the little cannon shown in the left-hand corner of this one was clearly based on reality. The barrel is held in a large block of wood that could be raised or lowered with pegs.

There were many reasons why knighthood declined toward the end of the Middle Ages. Archers began to replace knights as the "elite" on the battlefields, while new weapons like steel-armed crossbows, gunpowder, cannons, and eventually handguns made the heavily armored knight seem ineffectual.

The main cause of the knights' decline was the fact that western European civilization was changing and the feudal knight was now out of date.

In the 15th century, Swiss infantry defeated heavily armored cavalry knights so regularly that they helped undermine the whole prestige of the knightly elite. Even the best-equipped Austrian and Burgundian knights seemed unable to deal with Swiss mountaineers armed with crossbows, handguns, and heavy-bladed halberds (a combined spear and ax).

THE PEACEFUL KNIGHT

The change from military knight to village landlord and local keeper of the peace happened first in England. There were civil wars and rebellions, but during the 14th and early 15th centuries English armies did most of their fighting in other countries, particularly in France and the Netherlands.

Even in England a knight's younger sons often became soldiers, or mercenaries, or priests, since it was the eldest brother who inherited the family estate. As a result most of the leading soldiers were still knights, even if most knights were not soldiers. Knights were still the commanders of most armies.

Some huge cannons were made for siege warfare in the 15th century. One of the biggest was called "Mons Meg," which is now kept in Edinburgh Castle, in Scotland. Such giant guns were not, of course, used in open battle, where lighter forms of artillery were already threatening the future of the heavily armored knight.

KNIGHTS UNDER THREAT

Even after the knights' military position had been undermined by full-time professional soldiers, the knights tried to stay part of the ruling class. However, in the 14th and 15th centuries, merchants and bankers, and even farmers, were getting richer than the knights.

At this time, kings and emperors needed cash to pay mercenary armies, because professional soldiers usually wanted money for their services, not land fiefs or honors. The knights soon found that they were losing their power and influence to rich merchants and bankers who were loaning money to the kings and emperors.

A CODE OF CHIVALRY

One way in which knights tried to hold on to their superior social position was to live extravagant and colorful lives. They wore elaborate clothes and jousted in expensive tournaments where non-knightly "commoners" were not allowed to take part, no matter how rich they might be. The traditional codes of chivalry, in which a knight put "honor" above all things, had faded into a sort of dream. The lifestyle of a knight had become an expensive habit that ultimately ruined many knightly families who felt they had to take part to prove they were still the best.

The threat from crossbows and hand-held guns forced the craftsmen of 15th-century western Europe to make this full plate armor (right). Lighter than the mixed mail-and-plate protection of the 14th century, it allowed a fit man to run, jump, and even do somersaults!

45

KEY DATES AND GLOSSARY

The Middle Ages were a time of great turmoil in Europe. The armies of Popes, emperors, kings, and barons fought each other for control of land and cities, and there were also wars between Christian knights and their non-Christian enemies.

By the end of the Middle Ages, jousting tournaments took place, in some odd places, and for some strange reasons. There were even jousts on Old London Bridge. Sometimes whole teams would dress up as Turks, Saracens, Moors, pagan Greek gods, or even monsters. This military pageantry was all very different from the grim and dangerous military training of the 12th century

800 Charlemagne, king of the Franks, crowned as Holy Roman Emperor. His soldiers become the first knights.
911 A band of Vikings are given the Duchy of Normandy to rule and settle (from then on called Normans).
955 Knights of Otto I of Germany defeat invading Magyars (Hungarians) at Battle of Lechfeld.
1066 Normans conquer England.
1071 Battle of Manzikert, Byzantines defeated by Turks.
1073 Start of major political conflicts between Popes and Western Emperors.
1096–1100 First Crusade conquers Jerusalem (1099), creation of crusader states in the Middle East (Holy Land).
1147–1148 Second Crusade.
1173 New German expansion eastward.
1187 Saracen ruler Saladin defeats the crusader states and retakes Jerusalem.

1189–1192 Third Crusade.
1204 Fourth Crusade captures Byzantine capital of Constantinople.
1215 Magna Carta: King John makes political concessions to English barons.
1240 Mongol armies conquer Russia.
1241 Mongols invade eastern and central Europe. Teutonic, German, and Polish knights defeated at Battle of Liegnitz. Hungarian army defeated.
1242 Teutonic Knights defeated at Battle of Lake Peipus.
1250 Collapse of Western Emperor's power in Germany and Italy.
1300 Mercenary armies becoming more common, especially in Italy.
1326 Drawing of early cannon appears in European manuscript.
1337 Start of Hundred Years' War between England and France.
1348 Black Death (plague) ravages Europe.
1380 Lithuania accepts Christianity.
1415 England renews war with France, Battle of Agincourt.
1453 English expelled from France (except Calais), end of Hundred Years' War.
1492 Spaniards conquer Muslim Granada, end of the Reconquista.
1798 Knights Hospitallers surrender Malta to Napoleon Bonaparte.

Glossary

armorer: craftsman who makes armor.

Carolingian: ruling dynasty descended from Charlemagne.

chainmail: form of armor consisting of many rings linked together.

chansons de geste: epic poems of heroic deeds.

coat of arms: heraldic pattern used by an individual or a family.

coif: head-covering, either of chainmail as a form of armor, or of cloth for civilian use.

conrois: close-packed unit of knights.

courtly love: ideal of love between a knight and his lady, expressed in terms of brave actions, music, and poetry.

couched: held tightly under the armpit.

destrier: specially bred war-horse.

feudal system: economic system in which the military elite protected the peasants in return for food and taxes.

fleurs-de-lys: heraldic flower, badge of the French royal family.

hauberk: chainmail coat, early form of armor.

heraldry: recognized system of colors and patterns used in coats of arms.

illuminated: decorated with pictures.

land fief: piece of land or estate, given by a lord in return for military service.

mangonel: stone-throwing siege engine.

melée: "free-for-all" combat between two groups, units, or teams of cavalry.

mercenary: soldier hired for money.

Military Orders: religious order recruited from trained knights, similar to monks, but serving as elite troops.

militia: part-time soldiers, usually raised from the citizens of a town or city.

minstrel: singer, poet, and song-writer who popularized romantic ballads.

money fief: source of income given by a ruler to a knight instead of a fief.

Peace of God: one of several movements started by the Church in the 11th century to bring law and order back to chaotic parts of western Europe.

penance: penalty or form of sacrifice imposed by the church on a sinner.

plate armor: armor made from relatively large, rigid pieces of metal.

pommel: the knob at the end of a sword hilt or handle, or raised front of a saddle.

Saracen: medieval name for an Arab rather than a Turkish Muslim.

squire: lowest rank of noble society, often a young man who has not been knighted.

stirrups: metal loops into which a horseman puts his feet.

Quotations

Most of the quotations are taken from medieval histories called chronicles, or from poems. The challenge to single combat on page 23 was made during the Hundred Years' War between England and France. The oath on page 36 was made by a new recruit to the Order of Teutonic Knights. The quotation on page 43 is from the records of Genoa's legal advisor in the Black Sea port of Kaffa.

INDEX